duo

POETRY BY WOMEN

Published by Linen Press, London 2024
8 Maltings Lodge
Corney Reach Way
London W4 2TT
www.linen-press.com
© Linen Press 2024

The right of Linen Press to be identified as the author of this work has been asserted by her in accordance with the Copyright, Designs and Patents Act 1988.

Editors: Rosie Pundick with Jane Edberg, Avril Joy, Lynn Michell, Jess Richards.

Individual poems remain the copyright of the poet.

All rights reserved. This book is sold subject to the condition that it shall not, by way of trade or otherwise, be lent, resold, hired out, or otherwise circulated without the publisher's prior consent in any form of binding or cover other than that in which it is published and without a similar condition, including this condition, being imposed on the subsequent purchaser.

A CIP catalogue record for this book is available from the British Library.

Cover design: Lynn Michell
Cover image: Unsplash
Typeset by Zebedee
Printed by Lightning Source
ISBN: 978-1-7394431-3-9

CONTENTS

THE ORANGE-AND-WHITE HIGH-HEELED SHOES Ellen Bass	7
THE FIRST STEP IN WRITING A POEM ABOUT FEARS IS TO MAKE A LIST Monica Dobos	8
MY NAP Abigail Thomas	9
WHEN MY COLLEGE ROOMMATE VISITED PERU Joanne Durham	10
MY MOTHER, THE SEA Linda France	11
WOMEN COOKING CHICKEN Ruth Mota	12
THE SWEETNESS Laura Ann Reed	13
FIRST POMEGRANATE Alison Stone	15
PUBESCENT GIRLS FALL IN LOVE WITH WATER BALLET Merna Dyer Skinner	17
THE TRACK THE WHALES MAKE Marjorie Saiser	19
THE POWER OF BATHING SUITS Belinda Rimmer	20
RIDING LOGOS WAVES Shelly Eyre Graham	21
GEMINI Marilyn Longstaff	23
AZTEC LOVE SONG FOR WOMEN IN PRISON Avril Joy	24
MY SISTER'S FACE Brenda Najimian Magarity	25
A DREAM ABOUT MY MOTHER Cynthia Bernard	26
SUNDAY MORNINGS Brenda Najimian Magarity	28
ODE TO DR. LADD'S BLACK SLIT SKIRT Ellen Bass	30
ODE TO MY FRIEND, ALLYCE Eve West Bessier	32
FINAL POEM FOR AN ESTRANGED FRIEND Andrea Potos	34
HOMAGE TO MY LATIN TEACHER Linda France	35
STIGMATA ODE TO A CHILDHOOD FRIEND Jane Edberg	36
PARTS OF FLOWERS Rachel Burns	38
IN THE SEGREGATION UNIT Avril Joy	39

ASTRONOMY Dara Yen Elerath	40
INDIGO Ellen Bass	41
LUX PERPETUA Barbara Crooker	43
PARIS, CHRISTMAS 2016 Stephanie Powell	44
THE SISTERS PLAY CARDS IN A SNOWSTORM Marjorie Saiser	45
FRAILTY Lizzie Purkis	46
FROM 530 VANANDA AVE Mistee St. Clair	48
FEAR AND RAPTURE Mary Anne Smith Sellen	49
THE WIND FROM THE SIERRA Wendy Robertson	50
THE WAITING ROOM Mary-Jane Holmes	51
THE COLOR OF THE SKY Andrea Hollander	52
MISSING YOU AS I DO Mare Heron Hake	53
NAOMIE Stephanie Barbé Hammer	54
DIANA, WAKE UP Bonnie Hearn Hill	55
A CONVERSATION WITH SYLVIA PLATH Reshma Ruia	57
ON BOTTICELLI'S PRIMAVERA Mary-Jane Holmes	58
THE FOURTH BRONTË SISTER Beatriz F. Fernandez	59
LITTLE DARTS Laura Foley	60
NEW ME: MOTHER ME Reshma Ruia	61
WEB ADVICE: ELIMINATE EVERY FRICTION POINT YOU HAVE IN YOUR LIFE! Laurel Szymkowiak	62
HOW TO MAKE A GRANDMA Dragana Lazici	64
RELATIVITY Renée M. Schell	65
BRIGHTON BEACH Rebecca Faulkner	66
DUTY Yvonne Leach	67
HOW TO HELP A FRIEND MOURN Deborah Leipziger	68
COLD SOLACE Anna Belle Kaufman	70
LAUNCH Nicole Schnitzler	72
IN A PAINTING BY VERMEER Avril Joy	73

ROAD TO WINDSOR Ann Cefola	74
SELF-ELEGY Joanne Durham	75
WALKING WITH DOT Marilyn Longstaff	77
DURING THE PANDEMIC I LISTEN TO THE JULY 26, 1965, JUAN-LES-PINS RECORDING OF *A LOVE SUPREME* Ellen Bass	78
MEDICINE WOMAN Linda France	80
NEW LOVE: A LIST Jess Richards	81
POETS	83
ACKNOWLEDGEMENTS	93

THE ORANGE-AND-WHITE HIGH-HEELED SHOES

Today I'm thinking about those shoes—white
with a tangerine stripe across the toe and forceful orange heels—

that fit both my mother and me. We used to shop like that—
trying them on side by side. That was when there still

was a man who would cradle your heel in his palm
and guide your foot. Sometimes he would think he made a sale,

only to have one of us turn to the other—
and he would have to kneel again, hoping to ease another naked sole

into the bed of suede or leather. I thought those shoes
were just the peak of chic. And—my God—

she bought me a pair of orange cotton gloves to complete the ensemble.
Why is there such keen pleasure in remembering?

You are dead ten years. And these showy slippers—
we wore them more than half a century ago. The first boy

had not yet misted my breasts with his breath
and you were strong as a muscled goddess, gliding nylons

over your calves, lifting your amplitude into a breastplate.
Who will remember these pumpkin-colored pumps

when I die, too? Who will remember how we slid into them
like girls diving into a cedar-tinged lake, like bees

entering the trumpet of a flower, like birds disappearing
into the green, green leaves of summer?

Ellen Bass

THE FIRST STEP IN WRITING A POEM ABOUT FEARS IS TO MAKE A LIST

heights
mormon dentists
villain-elles
words that don't exist in English but they should
like *mestrina*, a moustache worn by middle-aged women
against their own accord
bunions—
although onions are fine
especially red, soaking in olive oil
drizzled with balsamic vinegar
bushy, red-headed beards
Dijon mustard—where it lands
leprechauns—what they tell you in dreams
my son calling me a bad mother if I get a divorce

The second step is crossing out all fears you
you will never write about:

high-heeled, fishnet stockinged legs
airport parking lots—I thought I left it on M?!
meeting new people—what they hold in their hearts
sestinas
swallowing my tongue in sleep
breaking mayonnaise—my sister always tells me
avoid olive oil, so good for your hair, though
getting lost in Fresno
making a blunder in oral—English
forgetting Romanian
my accordion heart at night
not being able to write a poem ever again
dying alone in a tiny house and I own a cat.

Monica Dobos

MY NAP

I poured my imagination through my left ear into a bowl on the nightstand hoping for a dreamless nap but as I might have known, it spilled over the sides and streamed onto the floor where every kind of tiny fish began to jump and gasp--leaving me high and dry so it could do as it wanted-- and soon there was a sea turtle, a baby walrus, three penguins, a couple of clams while I slept on dreamless, but I know the trouble you went to because when I began to wake the ocean whisked itself back into the bowl with an impossibly tiny splash and then into my ear, leaving fish all over the floor but taking everything else with it, and I saw you just as you were coming towards me naked and beautiful. Really. I'd know you anywhere. You could have just knocked.

Abigail Thomas

WHEN MY COLLEGE ROOMMATE VISITED PERU

she brought me back a two-inch figurine
of a llama. Surely female – though no
bronze or metal souvenir has testicles

or a penis to define it, I claimed
this one as a woman. Grayish brown,
with gold streaks defining fur on ears/

neck/belly, light reflected from the artist's
toothpick strokes. Her top side darker, I suspect
time has tarnished her. She still holds

her head erect, throat lifted, legs
balanced. A saddle humps her body,
but not her will. I've kept her all these years,

long after the miniature marble elephant
cracked, the origami cranes lost their folds.
Not much seems to harm the llama. Dust

clutches the bottom of her feet and laces
her ears, easily wiped away. Was she really
gold to begin with? What if after all

she was cast in feathers, not fur? Maybe
she's a flying llama, about to spring off
from bent knees. Is that what Kathi meant

to bring back to me – to assure us
our futures would be strange and wild
and satisfying? Would she be surprised

I still trace the contours of the llama –
and our friendship, that slipped
away as quietly as the dust?

Joanne Durham

MY MOTHER, THE SEA

Let me tell you a secret about
my mother. She was a mermaid who wore
lipstick, bloody as sea anemones
underwater. She sat all day on a rock
combing her naturally auburn hair
and never had to go to work. She knew
where all the treasure chests lay buried
so she didn't give a whelk about money.

Because she was a mermaid she made
children in secret, with no pain; sent them
to school with the fishes, taught them how to
eat oysters in any month with a moon
to row them home. She was courted by Neptune
and Hollywood but much preferred knitting.
O her nets were the talk of the ocean!
Fine as spray and spindrift, flossed with fine pearls.

And I'm proud to be one of her daughters –
the way I swim so strong, length by length
the City Pool. My breaststroke's the envy
of dolphins. The scales of my skin match
her own. But now she's gone full fathom five
all I have left are her stories I knit
into patterns like wide blue waves I dive
into, never once coming up for air.

Linda France

WOMEN COOKING CHICKEN

How unlike the chicken of my youth these skinless thighs and breasts
severed and tightly wrapped in cellophane labeled *organic and cage-free*.
Spared the sight of blood and scent of ripened flesh
I need nothing but a quick hot-wash to plop my pullet in the pan.

At thirteen, my first chicken came without a pedigree
blanketed in plain pink paper from Ducca's Butcher Shop.
I stood confronted by a whole chicken, except for head and feet
and pulled feathers that left her skin erupting just like mine.

I laid her naked on her back across the cutting board
shoved my hand through the viscous hole between her legs
to retrieve her heart her twisted neck, whatever *giblets* were.

My mother put me to this task without instruction
so my blade landed dull false cuts before I clipped her joints
divided up the body parts I dusted and dunked in sizzling oil.

So many million women in the world have washed the fat of chicken from their fingers.
I once saw a sugar-cane farmer's wife on a plantation in Brazil
chase a chicken with her machete to slit its throat.
She wrapped her legs ribboned with purple veins
around a bucket of scalding water to pluck its feathers.
That tough old hen who pecked for scratch would never sizzle in a frying pan
but boil for hours to flavor soup to feed a dozen kids.
Its beak and claws afloat, yesterday's bread sopping up its juice.

As I lay my platter down now upon my table
and watch my daughters' greasy fingers fiddle with crispy thighs and breasts
I wonder how, when they are women, they will relate to chickens?
Will they find it too grotesque to touch such flesh, let alone consume it?
Or will a uniformed woman wrapping in a factory make their slaughtered poultry palatable?

Ruth Mota

THE SWEETNESS

My grandfather peels cellophane wrap
from a fresh pack of Camels,
taps one out, lights up,
and blows a perfect orbit above my head.
I rise on my toes and reach
toward a form that blurs
and disappears.

Why didn't your sister come with you
on the boat? Where did she go?
In the windless heat and deep shadow
of a California orange grove,
his weathered hand gestures at the heavy farmer's boots
that replaced a music stand. I glance down
at his feet, hoping for a glimpse
of my great-aunt's face.
But all I see is dust
and a dust-choked
jimson-weed.

How long did it take
to get here from Odessa? Is it true,
what my mother says, that you brought
only those Yiddish songs you wrote?
He goes into the house and comes out
carrying a card-table and two folding chairs.
He sets up his chessboard in the green shade
of a citrus tree and darts from chair

to chair, playing against himself.
He doesn't cheat. I watch him
nudge a knight, a queen. Grandpa,
when you were my age, did you laugh?
Did you dance? He swivels in his seat
and plucks a Valencia orange
that hangs on a branch behind his back.
He strips the rind with his pocket knife
and hands me a piece of fruit.

I eat it all, meat, pith, seeds—
the way the earth ate my grandfather's life,
his sister's. The way it will eat mine.
Juice streams down my chin. My eyes sting
from the sweetness.

Laura Ann Reed

FIRST POMEGRANATE

Which part of this crimson
honeycomb to eat? And how? Sun
highlights the knife's blade, stripes the room
like prison bars.

I watch you scoop seeds, then copy;
savor sweet-tart bursts
as red pearls open.
Your food soothes me, your kind,
scratched-by-smoke-and-whiskey voice.

You must meditate, Sweet Pea.
Learn to let go. You're just like me
at that age – beautiful and charming,
far too stubborn.

Not with you.
I read the Trungpa books
you lend me, obey
traffic signs, take vitamins.

Juice stains your lips.
Suddenly clumsy, I spill
water, lose my spoon in the shag
rug. I've had offers, always thought
I didn't fancy women.
     Your blond hair.
                   Your breasts.
No one is that heterosexual.

Now I understand why my ex-boyfriend
sucked a chain of bruises down my neck
the first time I said yes.
Not passion, possession.
"Friend" is a pallid word.
Mentor, motherish though not kin,
I have no way
to mark you mine.
This jaundiced light's

too bright. It slices
my hand as I dig in the devoured
pomegranate's rind for hidden seeds.
Your husband
due back soon.
   Your voice, your hair.
                        My hunger.

Alison Stone

PUBESCENT GIRLS FALL IN LOVE WITH WATER BALLET

Like a lover's touch
we've yet to imagine—
the pool's warm water glides
beneath our necks,
slides along our arms, brushes
our downy-haired thighs,
our feet flutter kicking
just enough to keep us afloat.

You and I,
best friends,
partners in a summer swim class,
unafraid
to submerge ourselves,
to innocently spread our legs
into a V shape above the waterline,
slip into our favorite move—
the rotating sea-plank.

Floating, face-up,
head to feet,
you grab my ankles,
pull me forward—
as your body slips below mine
I pass over you, then catch
your ankles, guide
your body
over mine.

Again, and again
we move over and under—
only a sliver of water between us,
only ankles and palms touching—

Initiates of intimacy,
that summer
we discover the heat of boys'

lips touching ours,
fumbling fingers
awakening self-consciousness,
compelling us to measure
breasts, calculate each other's
hips-to-tits ratio.

Never do we anticipate
how years will slide one
into another, how
we will glide past one another
—through
   colleges,
   careers,
   kids—
how so many
men will pull us apart,
pass over us—
how our bond born from water,
a mooring of boat and anchor,
will link us always
—palms open

Merna Dyer Skinner

THE TRACK THE WHALES MAKE

You and I in the boat notice
the track the whales make,
the huge ring their diving draws
for a moment on the water.
I want to believe
when we can no longer
walk across the room
for a hug, can no longer
step toward the arms of the other,
there will be this:
some delicate trace that stays,
while below, out of sight,
dark mammoth shadow
flick of flipper
body of delight
diving deep.

Marjorie Saiser

THE POWER OF BATHING SUITS

In the clingy heat of a day trip,
my friend kissed me.
I chased her across pebbles,
then spinning and rolling into the waves.

On the train home,
to the growl and gallop of wheels,
we pressed our hot faces to the glass,
watched the world speeding past
and dreamt of hidden corners.

Now my friend is too sick
to mention kissing.

I harvest rhubarb from her garden,
bake crumbles, pies, jams, compotes.
Between sleeps, she licks pink strands from her lips,
saying, s*end food parcels to wherever I am gone.*

She gives me her cuckoo clock
to hang above my desk. It chimes
often and beyond the tick of hours,
not a *soft spontaneous shock**
but a reminder of sorrow.

I can recite it back pitch perfect,
me *cuckooing* into the still air.

Belinda Rimmer
*from Wordsworth's poem, The Cuckoo-clock.

RIDING LOGOS WAVES

emerging
from mama earth
through eons of bloom and
birth, people told me i came from
his rib (all xx chromosomal evidence
to the contrary) though i heard a
different sacred story from a
serpent so i ate the apple
took the blame
wore the fig leaf
kissed the frog who
did *not* turn into a prince
followed the frog back to the bog
where he wanted to stay on the surface
even as he grew extra legs after they invented
pesticides and being at a bit of a loss i slept with eyes
open for many years until i was kissed awake by such longing
for depth that i sank down under the whole ocean
to the bottom of the Marianna trench where
i sat awhile, drifting with snailfish and
other beings of salt water dream
in luminous darkness until
one day i remembered i
was an emergent
property of
the universe
with all its eternal
seamless sentience and i
forgave human ignorance
(not our fault) and reached back
to dear mama earth on seeing how i
fell from grace because of some crazy story
about separation, sin, shame and other weird shit
and how grateful i became to remember i am
a fleeting blossom born of essential oneness
and in the wake of that remembering
i fell back into innocence also
known as the garden, also
known as love, also

known as *her*
from whom
i came &
where i
belong

Shelly Eyre Graham

GEMINI

I signed a contract with myself
after my last major falling.
The wayward, brave, foolhardy me,
my passionate, reckless twin,
I wrapped in purple velvet and fuchsia silk,
incarcerated her at the bottom of
my sailor's oak chest at the foot of my
marriage bed, placed blankets on top
for smothering.

In Autumn, she settles a little with the
earlier and earlier drawing of thick curtains.
In Winter, she's dormant and I'm happy
in front of a blazing fire, hibernating.
I never let her out, although in Spring,
when the sap's rising, she rattles the lid and
itches my skin, humming a half-remembered
ditty, an earworm she's planted to make me
restless, scratchy.

Marilyn Longstaff

AZTEC LOVE SONG FOR WOMEN IN PRISON

I carry them to your house on my back,
uprooted flowers.
I am bent double with the weight of them,
of women torn from the soil, their roots mud
stem and sepal crushed
I carry them.

I carry their scent, the scent of ash
and blood in my blood.
Bent double with the weight of their fragility,
buds unopened, roses full-blown
discarded, trampled on
I carry them.

Their flower faces sit, geranium,
harebell, meadow-sweet,
in my classroom,
foliage fluttering in the breeze
from a barely open window
I carry the leaf of them,

bent double with the weight
of what we do to them,
how we punish and incarcerate,
condemn to iron fallen blossom, uprooted
flowers I carry them
on my back, to your house.

Avril Joy

MY SISTER'S FACE

In your face,
I read father's garden
where tomatoes, peppers
and eggplant abide in harmony.

Growing up,
we watched him rake and hoe
until the earth
loosened her veil
and welcomed his hands
to guide seed and plant
into place.

Since you have been ill,
a sorrowful cloud hovers overhead.
Resigned,
the rake leans against the shed
watching the hoe long for summer's sun.

In your face
I read Father's garden.

We wait
until he may once again
fulfill
the earth's thirst
for water.

Brenda Najimian Magarity

A DREAM ABOUT MY MOTHER

My mother is a barren field that somehow managed to have children.

    I am in the passenger seat.

Some mothers give birth, then take, take, take.

    My mother is behind the wheel.

Some mothers fall into tar pits of depression and linger there.

    The car is moving as if it's having a seizure, jerking and weaving. Accelerating.

Some mothers are furious volcanoes— you never know when they will erupt.
Some mothers are distant ice-storms; there's no mother there at all.

    There are children playing in the road.
    Balls, jump ropes, a plastic bat.

Some mothers make very small lives and then live them.

    She is holding up a newspaper in front of her face.

Some mothers tell many lies, new lies that fail to cover old lies.

    Her feet press the pedals at random. She is laughing.

I have had each of these mothers, sometimes.
Other times, none.

    I am trying to steer. So many children!

Now my mother has aged into a repulsive kind of old—
sits and complains, eats junk, grows ever more obese
on sugar-coated untruths about the past.

    I can't reach the brakes.

She's almost dead, having never really lived.

Am I doomed to live this way forever?

Cynthia Bernard

SUNDAY MORNINGS

(for my father, Paul)

I am eleven, your fourth and last child
and a girl, but it doesn't matter.

Sunday mornings belong to us.
You tousle me out of bed before sunup,
And we drive miles into the country.

You hunt while Pharaoh, the black lab
and I retrieve the doves you shot

Mornings,
where today a hunter mistakes
me for your son, and I am proud.

Then later, I carry a wounded
dove back to you its heart
beating in my hand,
and I am perplexed
by how one as magnificent as you
could cause any creature to suffer.

I know now that I will
never make a hunter,
but I don't speak of that
to you.

Mornings,
we go mushroom hunting
in the foggy woods.
You know the trees that wait
for us with their heavy burdens,
and you pare them
from their trunks.

We take them home,
chop the succulent masses
into pieces, and cook

them in garlic and sesame seed oil.
You tell me that when I turn sixteen,
I can get a hunting license.
You have a rifle just for me.

I nod agreement
while we eat the morning's find.

Sunday mornings
with you and me and the dog
and the sun rising over our heads
like a bucket full of laughter.

Brenda Najimian Magarity

ODE TO DR. LADD'S BLACK SLIT SKIRT

Praise to the little girl whose grandmother taught her to embroider,
slip the tip of the needle through the taut cloth and scallop the clouds,
fasten the feathers to bluebird wings.

And praise to the student who gulped muddy coffee
and memorized maps of muscles, puzzle of bones,
slid tendons through their shafts, curling and uncurling
each finger of the corpse like a deft puppeteer.

When I got to the ER Janet lay there, the morphine
not strong enough to blunt the pain.
Her arm looked like a carcass where a lion had fed.

Praise Dr. Ladd pulling green scrubs over her head
and gathering her long hair under a cap.

All the days we drove up to Stanford and waited for hours
in the room with the ugly orange carpet,
thumbing through tarnished pages of *National Geographic*,
wondering what Dr. Ladd would be wearing,
until we heard the strike of her high heels on the hallway linoleum,
distinctive as the first notes of Beethoven's Fifth.

Praise her hands that lifted Janet's hand, her fingertips brushing
the gnarled scars, flesh lumped like redwood burl.

Praise her for getting up early to outline her eyelids,
slick her lips. And praise to her blouses, the silk creamy
as icing on a cake, the generous buttons open
like windows in summer. And praise

her bracelets coiled gold and her wide leather belts
encircling her waist like two strong hands about to lift her.
Praise to her earrings, little jangling tambourines
and her perfume that braced us like a dry martini.

But most of all, praise to her slim black skirt
with the slit up the front so that when she sat down
and crossed her legs, the two panels parted like the Red Sea

and we were seized by the curve of her calves,
the faceted shine of her knees sheathed in sheer black mesh,
a riff of diamonds rippling up her thighs.

Ellen Bass

ODE TO MY FRIEND, ALLYCE

She is birds,
the way morning isn't morning
without them.

She is tender and steady
as the curving of leaves
toward light.

She is a beach comber,
a mother of children,
the way children are children
even when they are mothers
of children.

She is a wind chime sounding
in a subtle distance,
a light caring over faces,
an evening's thoughts
sifted from a day.

She is a moving,
the way air changes
when it passes,
soothing and wearing,
the way a current
is transparent
over other currents,

a layering of essentials.

The way I can believe
the mystical
is naive
of its mysticism.

The way we do not own ourselves.

The way of seasons
and of tides,

and of memories
of seasons

and of tides
and of memories.

Eve West Bessier

FINAL POEM FOR AN ESTRANGED FRIEND

for S.

My last dream had me chasing you
along some narrow stone path rising and twisting
on a Greek island mountainside
while I screamed at you to finally believe
I had not wronged you. Still,
you kept your righteous gait.

I awoke exhausted from all
my efforts, recent and past,
decided I must rest.
I remembered, in the dream,
in the darkness beside me lay the Mediterranean
sea of my ancestors, lapis and deep
and dazzling by daylight--
water that knew my innocence.

Andrea Potos

HOMAGE TO MY LATIN TEACHER

(for Mrs Stanley Hall)

You swept into the lesson, dressed in red,
chalk dust powdering your patrician nose,
already translating Parkstone Grammar
First Form into AD 43:
our first taste of your noble, passionate tongue.

Salvete puellae! And we'd chant back
Salve domina! The exclamation mark
a chorus of chairs scraping the tiled floor
as we sat, a fizzing cohort of girls.

You rolled the words around your mouth and sucked
the juice out of them. I hid at the back
and watched you spit. Like a mother bird,
you fed us from your own lips – *the table;
to the table; by, with, from the table.*

And so I learnt to unravel the puzzle
of the 'Unseen', marvel at the precision
of syntax and rhetoric, recognise
the English in the squares of the mosaic.

We could all have cheered at Cicero's coaxing,
wept when Dido flung herself on the pyre,
but knew that someone had to found Rome
or else we'd have no baths, no straight roads,
no alphabet from which to build our own.

Your daughter was in the year above mine.
I wondered how it would be to have you
as a mother; if you talked Latin at home.

Linda France

STIGMATA

Ode to a Childhood Friend

I sat on a bench unpicked
in the schoolyard new
to the country with my funny accent
and dumb boyish looking shoes.
No one wanted a strange stranger to kick
balls with. Then you sat down beside me,
long lanky limbed, hair down to your butt,
the most popular girl.

You saw my sad and wanted to make it better.

After school you took me
to your brother's trailer, we sat
at the foldout table mixing cocoa with mescaline,
stuffing capsules and licking our fingers.
When the sky went dark,
we lay in the back yard grass,
two astronaut girls riding crows to the moon.

I was so happy I cried, and you held me like a mother.

You said, 'When in the doghouse decorate.'
So, at midnight, we put on eyeliner and lipstick,
rolled our skirts up as high as we could.
We crammed pillows into your bed,
and snuck out the bedroom window
to hitchhike to a nightclub on the Sunset
Strip. I was twelve, you thirteen.
You had boobs and I had what your brother called
two fried eggs, sunny side up.
At the bar, grown men flirted, offering
us alcohol and bennies. They let us
sit at their booth, our naked legs dangling.

How did we survive when the Zodiac Killer was on a spree?

You once took me to the Renaissance
Faire located in an oak dotted glen,
dressed in long skirts, leather-laced push up corsets,
garlands of dried flowers in our hair.
At nightfall, the hippies gathered in the dark
woods dancing and howling. I learned how to
hold in a lung full of marijuana smoke
without choking. We dropped LSD and shared
the half-gallon bottle of cheap Spañada wine
you stole from your mother.
I said, 'I need to pee.'
You laughed and said, 'Jesus Christ, OK.'
So, I did. My skirt drenched.
While walking slant, the world
twirled paisley patterns beneath our bare feet.
We hitched a ride to your house where you held my head
above the toilet while I ralphed Buicks into the bowl.
You gently wiped my face with a cool wet rag.

I was always confused when your father took you in the back room.

I could hear you squealing, pleading
for him to stop. I wavered between jealous
of that undivided attention and terrified
that something was wrong.
You'd come out all red, eyes swollen, wiping away
tears with a smile on your face. I never asked you
what happened and you never told me.

It was 40 years later, over a bottle of wine,
you said, 'Those blessed
by good favor are those blessed
by God.' I knew you as an atheist, but now,
you made a beautiful catholic.
You spoke of marks, stains found
on hands, feet, head, and heart. You described your crippling
pain from rheumatoid arthritis, how you endured
47 surgeries to remove the disease you believed
were the sins of the father.

I thought you were talking about Jesus.

Jane Edberg

PARTS OF FLOWERS

We follow Sister Francis
through the cloisters,
past the stations of the cross.
The scent of flowers fills the chapel,
ovary, ovule, gynaeceum,
death and resurrection.

Your mother sends you back
to your former junior school.
Take your report to Sister Francis.
Don't you dare come home
until she's seen it. Your mother's spittle
on your face, like dark rain.

Peonies, dahlias and petunia.
Yellow star of Bethlehem.
Sepal, stamen, stigma.
You knock on the convent door.

Sister Francis is not home.
White dead nettle and dog rose.
Posterior and anterior lobe.
Vexillum, lateral, wing.

You run away to Roddymoor woods
make a bed from the branches of ash
pray until your palms sweat blood.
Your father's garden has fruit canes.
Redcurrants, bitter on the tongue.

The bearded man from Housing
reads your father's letter.
To whom it may concern.
Time burns slow.
Filament, anther, dioecious.
I disown her as a daughter.

Rachel Burns

IN THE SEGREGATION UNIT

I ask to see you,
they look at me like I've got religion
or some unwanted disease.
Still after all these years they refuse
to believe I am not one of them.

You want to go in there, see her?
You want me to unlock that door?

Yes. Please.

There are no mango trees in segregation,
no limbs growing one into another,
grafted on,
there is only separation
alone

you raise your eyes to greet me
then down at the cardboard potty on
the concrete floor, down
to your fancy dress strip-gown.
You cannot offer me a bed to sit on
or tea or mango juice.

There is only stone and the window so
high we might as well be far out in deep
space, the caged light our spaceship,
with its film of dead, black flies.

Avril Joy

ASTRONOMY

Eva and I used to sleep on the moon. We dreamed it was a sloop passing through the Atlantic, though we knew it was only a stone the color of bones and chalk. When Eva grew angry she'd lock the moon in a drawer so I could not see it; so I could not caress its cratered face, then I'd watch her chase it around the yard like a balloon. She'd bury it in the garden and moon trees would bloom that bore luminous fruit. When we ate the fruit our lips turned sticky, our teeth began to rot. Then our parents would hide the moon, telling us children should not play with such a precious toy. They did not know the moon was our only joy, our lantern, our mirror, our lake. It was the oven in which we'd bake our bread of sorrow and forgetting. Now we are alone and there is no bread, no fruit. Now, Eva and I root through the dark looking for something to spark us the way the moon once did. Sometimes, we find fireflies and seal them in jars; we know they are fake moons, their glow a false glow, but we are growing girls and need moonlight the way we need air. We need moonlight the way we need salt. At night, we dream we are moons docked to planet Earth; the world turns and we fly out into space. We trace the arcs of comets with their tails of light. We turn from girls into galaxies. We turn from children into stars.

Dara Yen Elerath

INDIGO

As I'm walking on West Cliff Drive, a man runs
toward me pushing one of those jogging strollers
with shock absorbers so the baby can keep sleeping,
which this baby is. I can just get a glimpse
of its almost translucent eyelids. The father is young,
a jungle of indigo and carnelian tattooed
from knuckle to jaw, leafy vines and blossoms,
saints and symbols. Thick wooden plugs pierce
his lobes and his sunglasses testify
to the radiance haloed around him. I'm so jealous.
As I often am. It's a kind of obsession.
I want him to have been my child's father.
I want to have married a man who wanted
to be in a body, who wanted to live in it so much
that he marked it up like a book, underlining,
highlighting, writing in the margins, I was here.
Not like my dead ex-husband, who was always
fighting against the flesh, who sat for hours
on his zafu chanting om and then went out
and broke his hand punching the car.
I imagine when this galloping man gets home
he's going to want to have sex with his wife,
who slept in late, and then he'll eat
barbecued ribs and let the baby teethe on a bone
while he drinks a dark beer. I can't stop
wishing my daughter had had a father like that.
I can't stop wishing I'd had that life. Oh, I know
it's a miracle to have a life. Any life at all.
It took eight years for my parents to conceive me.
First there was the war and then just waiting.
And my mother's bones so narrow, she had to be slit
and I airlifted. That anyone is born,
each precarious success from sperm and egg
to zygote, embryo, infant, is a wonder.
And here I am, alive.
Almost seventy years and nothing has killed me.
Not the car I totaled running a stop sign
or the spirochete that screwed into my blood.
Not the tree that fell in the forest exactly

where I was standing—my best friend shoving me
backward so I fell on my ass as it crashed.
I'm alive.
And I gave birth to a child.
So she didn't get a father who'd sling her
onto his shoulder. And so much else she didn't get.
I've cried most of my life over that.
And now there's everything that we can't talk about.
We love—but cannot take
too much of each other.
Yet she is the one who, when I asked her to kill me
if I no longer had my mind—
we were on our way into Ross,
shopping for dresses. That's something
she likes and they all look adorable on her—
she's the only one
who didn't hesitate or refuse
or waver or flinch.
As we strode across the parking lot
she said, O.K., but when's the cutoff?
That's what I need to know.

Ellen Bass

LUX PERPETUA

--and you, my friend, out there somewhere,
still ahead of us in the light. Christopher Buckley on Larry Levis
for Susan Elbe

A light that's glancing off the hickory leaves,
Midas-touched in the October sun. The world dims,
the dousing of a flame in the hearth. There's copper
and bronze in the trees, goldenrod lighting the meadows
and fields; squirrels are digging in, storing their hoard for the hard
days to come, and bees return to the hive, summer's sweetness
sealed in wax. The sky is still heartache blue, but November
is coming, with its afghan of gray, threaded by geese,
everything gone to seed. Sitting by the fire
with a tumbler of whisky, I raise a glass to you,
old friend. So many words unsung: flocks of birds
gathering in stanzas on telephone wires, ready to lift
into the endless blue at a moment's startle.

Barbara Crooker

PARIS, CHRISTMAS 2016

I wake up. Her foot in the harbour
    of my knee.

Delivering a thousand small kicks
   as though
   a newly caught fish
   slap-dying in air.

In the 20th Arrondissement
we share a bed
with a view of *parc de Belleville*.

This morning, wine bottles emptied
    into the Poubelles
    are a new violence.

Between rods of grey light
the debris of our twenties
washes up on the floor
the wet wipes, makeup tubes
rolled-up knickers, all glittering
trash, as anchorless as we are.

Julien's brother has trained
his cat to use the toilet –
piss champagnes into the bowl
every few hours.

On Boxing Day, she is depressed
and sits alone in the kitchen.

In bed I listen:
    amidst the crying
    nails on plastic
        the flow of urine louder than tears.

Now   we are laughing
    or dying, whatever.

Stephanie Powell

THE SISTERS PLAY CARDS IN A SNOWSTORM

The sister who can drive
picks up the others,
her car chugging in each driveway
while a sister steps out,
pulling her door shut behind her.
We have no business out in such a storm,
one says, laughing, no business at all.
But the wind takes her words and swirls them
like snow across the windshield. It's on to the next house,
the next sister. At the last house they play canasta,
the deuces wild, even as they were in childhood,
the wind blowing through the empty apple trees,
the shadows of bumper crops.
They're kids again, remembering their trick
on a salesman who came to their farmhouse:
We draped a sheet over Margaret's head—
Margaret was willing—our ghost
bobbing and moaning in the doorway
in broad daylight. We got rid of that one—
bring on the next one! We're rascals
sure as barnyard dogs.
The snow thickens, the coffee perks,
and nothing is lost if it can be retold.
We'll have to quit someday, one or the other says.
We're getting up there in the years. We'll have to quit,
but today—
deal, sister, deal!

Marjorie Saiser

FRAILTY

(For Brenda)

It was a door in a garden wall,
where the path ended, or began;
around its stone arch ivy flowed,
and bore a delicate climbing rose.

What made us pause?—a wish to stay
while the sun streamed into each
contented stone, to receive the afternoon
shade's soft-edged leaf print on our
faces, to hear the breeze slacken,
then intensely gather, to touch
the warm iron latch and wonder.

Watchful of the sun's angle,
our gathering thoughts stilled by the flight
of a cabbage white, softened by the shy
scent of the rose, we lingered.

    *   *   *   *

It is the brief alive pause,
the vine's unfailing hold,
that come back now. I stand
here reading uncertainly
how illness closes in on you,

feeling how much this warning
matters, but how, like shock's silent
surge, it shows only on the inside.
Response means crossing fields,
the almost insurmountable span
of fields that distance. I know
my presence would act against
fear of frailty—as if
to rest my hand on the latch,

feel the door freely yield,
see light adding to light,
the banks of lilies along the wall,
find myself, unfrozen, running
up the long meadow to your house.

Lizzie Purkis

FROM 530 VANANDA AVE

-The Sonoran Desert, for my grandmother

Each afternoon we sit on the porch and drink a beer,
stare at the Ajo range and listen to the wind
through her citrus trees and the mesquite,
the chirrups of quail. What she did five minutes ago
folds into yesterday and, forgetting
that she's already made three meatballs for her little black dog,
she sets out more, which attracts flies that land on us
with a tickle. The big ones are flesh flies, I believe.
I suppose anywhere there are humans,
these small beasts convene. We leave too much behind.
I am daydreaming of inheriting this house and keeping her
watercolors and brushes, the roadrunner pottery.
I'd walk early and look for javelinas
like we used to. Years ago,
we woke to the yipping howls of coyotes,
neither of us could sleep so, she in her recliner,
me flat on the couch, we listened in that darkness
I've only known in the desert. I'll never forget that.
A fly lands on my arm and grooms. A flesh fly
is one of the first to recycle death's nutrients
into this pale and hungry soil. If I had an open wound,
it might hatch maggots. But this wound doesn't exist yet,
and I suspect it would be uninhabitable. Someday
when I pull down a lemon or orange I'll inhale
not a loneliness, but some sort of quietness
I am learning to sense. This morning
I rubbed creosote oil on my wrists, my neck.
It smells like desert rain, zoetic and ancestral,
buried in deep earth and just released.

Mistee St. Clair

FEAR AND RAPTURE

(For Valentine Ackland and Sylvia Townsend Warner)

We are drawn here as though roped to the moon,
descending golden flanks of dunes to reach
the sea-creased sands. They hold the shape
and weight of our feet, our names.

The air is salt and urgent. It wraps us closely
in its rough, linen grasp, lifts our hair into
crests and pennants as we run to where the tide
bevels its smooth jade against the shoreline.

The heart has no horizons, there is no vanishing point
in its landscape. We hover at the brink of danger and ecstasy,
fear and rapture. Behind us, the past dissolves into a mirage.
Before us, uncharted oceans just waiting for our stars to align.

Valentine Ackland said that 'fear and rapture' were the predominant emotions of her childhood and continued to shape her life.

Mary Anne Smith Sellen

THE WIND FROM THE SIERRA

In the twilight of the ward
the old woman pulls me to her side
she whispers in the tight shell of my ear.
Her voice, dancing on a roaring tide,
surfs sixty years of life
with West Coast ease.
I let down my hair, she says, when I
was nursing in the Spanish War.
After the lice, the blood, the mucus-mud
of that First Conflagration –
many women cut their hair,
silky smooth to their skulls.
Not me! I treasured my locks.
Daytime on the ward, I wore my hair.
tightly bound, moulded to my head
like a Roman helmet. And every night
I brushed it out, tress by golden tress,
a miserly Rapunzel alone in my room.
Of course, I say, since that Spanish prelude
haven't we had our own wars here?
Not so much the innocence of fighting
face-to-face but cities raped, skies riven,
fire storms raging. Does this compare with
the Spanish cloth-capped anarchy all
fluttering flags and posters pitted innocently against
the tyranny of flying steel?
Later generations paid world rates for
learned arguments and justification -
the comfort of men in suits. Little comfort
for hearts being ripped out of cities and of citizens,
when the price of planes and bombs
was paid in flesh and pain and administered.
by medallioned clerks.
In the twilight of the ward
the voice in my ear is now a fading tide.
smelling of salt and iodine.
of Dettol and rotting fish.
My hair fell loose in Spain, she murmurs.
I liked to feel it lifting
in the warm wind from the Sierra.

Wendy Robertson

THE WAITING ROOM

On this island, there are trees that bear fruit like women, with shapes, bodies, eyes, hands, feet, hair, breasts, and vulvas like the vulvas of women. They are the most beautiful of face and hang by their hair...when they feel the wind and sun, they yell, 'Wāq Wäq, [help help] until their hair tears apart. When their hair tears, they die. Ibn al-Wardi (d. 1348 ce)

We sit – an atoll of women – gently
metastasizing like slow-to-ripen fruit
beneath the strip-lighted pulse
of this wave-filled coast, archipelago
of scan, x-ray, magnetic resonance.

In this forest's bloom, we wait, hollow
as calabash, thumbing mounds of Vogue
and other fabulas of paradise that recount
little of how to stem lava flows or build
boats out of small pieces of wood.

The world flits around us in coral scrubs
and Crocs, exotic birds singing out
our names, our date of birth, clocking
our descent in cubits of hair length
while we learn what it is to be marooned

to forever button, unbutton our clothes
until we are just a back-lit negative of tree
shadows on a chart, sum of our disposable
parts: stroma, lobule, areole, ovary, bone
lymph, breath, wind, sun, the roar of a full moon.

Mary-Jane Holmes

THE COLOR OF THE SKY

No matter what I tell you about the sky tonight,
even if I tell you everything I know
about its dark rich blue, faded here
and there like the velvet jacket my mother
used to wear, and how much I loved her
when she wore it, how much I loved to touch
her arm or think about touching it, how sometimes
I would even walk deep into the walk-in closet,
dark as the sky is tonight, and reach
and find it by touch, and know it, electrically,
the way I know your body in our bed at night,
in the black room of that room, way in the back
where no one could find me, in the blue
black night of that soft cave, and the smell of it,
the faded smell of my mother there and the way
I felt—all velvet and alone and blue myself, and
somehow safe, just safe. No matter what I tell you
about the color of the sky tonight, you will not know
enough about the sky at all, about its magnificent blue
that I know I could touch, that changes and disappears
no matter how much I say, no matter how much
I want it to stay.

Andrea Hollander

MISSING YOU AS I DO

if you were here, I'd take you to the mall
where I might buy the new pair of shoes
I really need and you'd help me choose
and then we'd wander around, probably holding
hands because you've been like that
for about ten years, starting up
again, in high school, after stopping
in the middle from childhood, and we'd laugh
at the funny slogan t-shirts and I'd look
at some of the bright jewelry but pass
on all of it, and then you'd want to go
to the one clothing store
for the bargains, and we'd read the signs
carefully on the colorful clothes
because the bargains bring you in
the door but it's a tricky store
that can cost a lot on the other stuff
when you least expect it, and then we'd walk like this,
just chatting, until we hit the food area
and we'd stop, as we always have,
for a soft pretzel that the doctor says
I can't eat, so I'd only have a few pieces
and we'd laugh just like before,
until we made our way back
outside, still probably touching,
linking our arms with our bags,
and we'd buy a fruit drink from a popular brand,
me with my off-pink drink and you with yours
until we leave the mall, our place
until next time, and add this treasure
of comfort thoughts for when we're feeling
too far apart, maybe not with the same season
or light or sunset, unable to touch
with anything but words
no matter how many things we buy.

Mare Heron Hake

NAOMIE

Was beautiful in a not immediately
Apparent sort of way
She came into the wine shop and said
I cut hair.
I was dubious. She seemed too good to
Be true, but she was. Good and true, that is.
He went to her and then I went
And she was a brilliant stylist
And the nicest person
Tell me what you know she said
When she found out I was a professor
So I told her things and she asked
Questions and read the books
I recommended, including
The ones I had written.
She's gone now – moved to
Idaho, and sometimes I walk
By her empty shop in the little
Downtown where I used to live:
The walls painted a blueish grey
And old hand mirrors hang from the wall
Embrace your beauty
Reads a placard.
I often find those sayings
Corny
But when I think of Naomie
I know she
Meant it;
a vision of her face
a snip of memory
falls onto the floor
not swept up:
a curl of the time
we spent together
lies here
for a truly good moment.

Stephanie Barbé Hammer

DIANA, WAKE UP

Hear me through the thick
cold walls, past the beeping
reality, past all of the noises,
the voices blurring your senses.

Diana, wake up.
Caterpillar clouds fill
the sky. Dry throats croak out
words without meaning.
Messages get lost,
translated into languages
neither of us speaks nor
understands, scrambled
like eggs.

Diana, wake up.
Know your name,
Mark's name.
Know mine.
Remember our plans,
a party in the fall,
Oktoberfest in the shotgun
backyard, the green lace
of bee's balm
bordering our music
as you dance.

Diana, wake up.
because the longer you stay
there, the more you'll forget
how to leave, the more
that place will start to feel
like safety and like home.
But it isn't.
We are safety.
We are home.

There's still time, Diana.
Wake up.

And when you do,
once we're sitting there
in your immortal kitchen
counting the years
and fears between us,
you will look at me
with those eyes
that miss so little,
and you will say,
"Were you going to
publish that poem if
I died?"

And I will tell you, no,
Diana.

Besides, you
are not going to die,
not on your life, Diana,
not in my poem.

Bonnie Hearn Hill

A CONVERSATION WITH SYLVIA PLATH

Her grave sulks on an ugly slope.
An untidy patch. There are brambles, dandelions too.
A foxglove peeps its head through the granite slab with its puckered ridges.
The wind is a wave in slow motion.
A shrine of sorts it is – this in-between world – for passing poets and women
who carry a carnival of chaos in their hearts and wombs.
Paper roses. A postcard. A child's rattle rusty gold. A wedding ring.
A photo of a smiling Ted.
His face buried in the nest of her bouncy gold hair
where a red ribbon blooms.
A drop of blood.

I lurk there with my empty hands.
I have nothing to offer.
She will speak soon. I wait.
The clouds bleat heavy with rain.
The church door is a clown's face streaked with tears.
Still I wait.
She is there. Not a pale ghost but made of ripe flesh.
The trick, she tells me, is to balance while falling.
To stand still while burning quick.

Reshma Ruia

ON BOTTICELLI'S PRIMAVERA

If we turn it on its head, look at poor cupid
thrashing his bingo-wings, arrow aimed not down
from Medici orange groves but upward out of rows
of what look like Boule d'Or, a hardy French turnip
(God bless a nation that has never heard of swede).
I bought a packet of the seeds once, not here
where Spring still spins her fretwork of frost,
but in a sunny Occitan *hammeau* where the women's talk
was of chanterelle and walnut harvests, the lack
of water in the cisterns, the children. *Your little ones?*
They asked, smoothing the polyester of their housecoats.

They took me then to a barren patch of ground, bent
to its stones, scooping the belly of the earth sunward, breasts
pendulous as peppers. We planted by the moon, garlic
and artichokes. By the planets: elecampane in Mercury,
motherwort in Venus. They taught me all their secrets:
pinching out the seventh leaf so the melon gave
its sweetest juices, how every plant has a perfect companion.
The garden swelled and those turnips —tops breaking
the surface like golden fontanelles.

Here, the gritter's amber flash turns dusk to night
as I rootle old coffee tins for what's left. Here
are those seeds now past their best. Outside
Zephyrus blows blue the March wind, pressing his hands
round the land's thin waist, lifting it, the hills as ballast.

Mary-Jane Holmes

THE FOURTH BRONTË SISTER

Emily Dickinson requested that her favorite of Emily Brontë's poems be read at her own funeral

Emily, my mirror reflects my own plain
white smock and tightly combed bun,
but I envision your moor-swept gray eyes
and wind-tangled black locks instead—
In your words, I found a haven beyond
my father's ground where we might meet.

If only we might have crossed the leagues
of ocean that moved between us—
how would we have greeted each other?
I imagine your hand, hard and stone-cold in mine,
our ink-stained fingers mingling—I
mute in your giant presence.

What new ground could our lips break
that we have not raked over so many times
with our pens? We who dared travel our twin
paths as margin-dwellers—dark outlanders
solemnly bordering others' busy-bright lives—
Like ash-blackened stones surrounding hearth fires,
perhaps we were meant to come together
only in the landscape we both shared.

Sisters in mind, sisters in pain, I see us together,
walking your heather-darkened trails,
your dog trotting along at your side,
even as my constant Carlo is ever at mine
within these four walls' soft shadows.

No coward minds, ours. In the end,
I wished your words to explode
like fireworks over the placid lake
of my grave, baptize my few mourners with flame—
as if your voice had spoken my name
and the broken earth itself gave answer.

Beatriz F. Fernandez

LITTLE DARTS

In the Winooski bank, a wispy-haired woman
in pink-flowered dress, matching pink purse,
forgets why she's there, explains her memory loss,

asks the teller to withdraw thirty dollars,
then forgets how much she's asked for,
as the teller nods, smiles, reminds.

I've driven two hours to this branch,
to close my late sister's account.
I carry her dark blue checkbook,

handwriting neat and legible, small numbers
added, subtracted, all I have left of her
enclosed in two Manila envelopes.

When she died, in her bathtub,
her new townhouse almost empty of furniture,
she must have known

she wouldn't be hosting anyone,
must have enjoyed the feeling
of owning so much private space.

At my turn in line, the bank manager
shakes my hand, looks into my eyes:
I'm so very sorry for your loss.

I wonder if she sees my old grief,
for a sister lost to me long before she passed,
snow-cold and distant as Pluto's furthest moon.

That night, I watch, from a lawn chair,
little darts of light, like us,
streaking and falling across a great darkness.

Laura Foley

NEW ME: MOTHER ME

I wake up this morning and become her. My mother.
Rushing to the toilet for a pee,
I grab the mirror to my face.
Something is wrong. Something is right.
The face staring back is hers alright.
I slip on my skirt. Pull up my tights.
Check the mirror again. The winter grey hair
sleeping on my head,
the sunken eye with its faded iris
once the lighthouse to my days.
They are hers.
My mother's disappointments. Her sighs.
A lifetime's blessing by my bedside.
I plunder them. I hug them tight.
Go out to meet the world
with a jagged smile
and a heart clenched like a boxer's fist.

Reshma Ruia

WEB ADVICE: ELIMINATE EVERY FRICTION POINT YOU HAVE IN YOUR LIFE!

When I find my husband's mother, Agnes
standing before the open refrigerator,
the defrosting ground beef already
nibbled down to a frozen lump, her
hand in last night's casserole, several
grapes squashed under her shoes, I
wrap black Velcro tape
through both refrigerator handles.

When I find Agnes wandering
through the house, a chunk
of bread in each hand, ripped
from the fresh loaf
tucked under her arm, when
I find Agnes chugging
balsamic vinegar from
the large cruet next to the sink,
when I find teeth marks
on unripe avocados
in a bowl, I clear the counters no cruets
no avocados/no bread/salt/
pepper/ half-filled coffee cups,
invoke St. Jude of the desperate and

embrace hypervigilance as my new life.

I secure dishes, pans, utensils behind
cupboard doors, wipe kitchen counter
of every crumb. I retighten
refrigerator Velcro, and hide away
koi food pellets, plant saucer pebbles,
tempting bright crayons, lock
the garbage pail in another room.
To be so vulnerable. Her. Me.

Each night I step outside, allow
the distant moon darkness to press into me,

whisper good night to the lonely bear
waiting for my dreams.

Laurel Szymkowiak

HOW TO MAKE A GRANDMA

ensure she is born during or after a war
so she can appreciate night sky tranquillity

make her sturdy and plain and give her a righteous vision
so she can complete housework under candlelight

teach her to be a seamstress so she can mend the silence
when she marries a green man from her village
who would prefer the bottle than to spend time with her

when she gives birth in the kitchen amidst the jars of pickles
warn her that she must survive
the starved days for her daughter

let her queue daily for rationed eggs and flour
so she learns about the exquisiteness of the dictator

teach her to fill stomachs with less than five ingredients
and that parsley solves all savoury dilemmas
– a hand sewn apron must be worn when cooking

provide her with a pig iron backbone
to carry on after her husband's heart attack

turn her into a stubborn widow
– she isn't a sea otter and doesn't need to hold hands

let her kiss her granddaughter's forehead
before they defect this land of paltry plums

and firmly remind her that a lady must always wear lipstick
when leaving the house no matter her age

Dragana Lazici

RELATIVITY

Reading the science magazine with my son,
I realize it's not the gravitational pull
that's so hard to comprehend

but the dead star so dense
no light can escape.

Like the sister I never had,
you wore the yellow bridesmaid's dress
at my wedding.

You massaged my back when the baby kicked
her way free of my body,

fed me slices of orange
while her newborn eyes
took in the ways of the world.

Relativity's not so much about time,
as though the hurt will be farther away

in ten or twenty years—but all that mass
compressed to the unfamiliar tone

in your voice, when I knew
you'd dropped our fourteen years
to a slippery place with no name.

To bend light you need a gravitational field
or a small child listening.

Renée M. Schell

BRIGHTON BEACH

when the cab hits 50 I am on the backseat
counting contractions as sunrise rips
through treetops in East River Park

breathing hard I am back at the club
where I held Jesse's hair   in the bathroom
the midwife takes my pulse

her too-thin wrists silver jangle   like Jesse's
that night we climbed stoplights
on Stanton   as my pitocin kicks in

Jesse's head on my shoulder
when we slept on the F   rode it out
to tomorrow   ate borscht

from chipped bowls   crimson
& cold   her breath sour from the pills
last night's heartbreak

on the boardwalk   Jesse showed me
the shape of her grief   how she slipped
beneath floorboards when her father

wiped o the blood   sandblown we skimmed
stones   opened up slowly   she told me
it was time   that I should push hard

my daughter was born the night
Jesse died   I hold her small wrists
blue eyes open like morning street lamps

Rebecca Faulkner

DUTY

The downstairs den glows with late-night TV.
My mother settles into *Doctor Zhivago*
after a day of caring for the six of us.

When I walk in with my lungs on fire
asthma clenches them into rattle and wheeze.
The room is full of air, air stretches through the house

and outside, above other houses
and as far as the moon.
But the right-in-front-of-me air wants

nothing to do with me.
And I see in my mother's expression
both sympathy and disappointment.

When air doesn't cooperate,
she leads me into the small bathroom,
moves the rug so I don't sit on cold tile,

and turns the squeaky knob for Hot all the way
to the right. Steam rises, misting the mirror first,
then clouds take the toilet, and soon

I am drenched in warm fog,
tracing water droplets with my finger
as they run jagged down the wall,

my other hand in my mother's hand.
In time, a strong breath pries open my lungs.
She gives me a squeeze, and then lets go.

Yvonne Leach

HOW TO HELP A FRIEND MOURN

Begin by baking a blueberry loaf.
For this you will need lemons.
You will need to plant a lemon tree.
Grow it in an arid place.
Collect the lemons in woven baskets.

Gather the blueberries as you did when you were little
when your daughters were little.
You remember – early in the morning, before the heat.
Running the wild
blueberries through your fingers.

Let the scent of lemons perfume
your hands,
penetrate your pores.

Grate the lemons and then
collect the lemon juice.
Zest first then juice the warm sun of the lemon.
The lemons will resemble a shell,
hollowed out.

Remember, this is a cake that needs tending.
On this cold November night, the butter will be a brick.
Soften it. Slowly. Take whatever means necessary.
Remember that baking is coaxing.

Beat the sugar crystals into the butter
until they resemble snow, circles of snow,
snow rocks.

Add the lemon juice, zest, vanilla.
Stem the tide of panic when you notice
the flour is nearly finished. Feel the gratitude
for the second
bag wedged deep into the pantry.

Add the eggs, one by one, and watch them
dissolve into the snow. Add flour and slowly,
the gritty almond flour.

Forgive yourself the small transgression,
the vanilla pooling on the counter. A pond.

You are making clouds.
Watch them form and cluster.
Watch the clouds absorb the blueberries
slowly sinking, submerged.

Bake the cloud loaf
but tend to it.
Lower in more blueberries.
Watch them dot the top of the loaf, no longer
sinking.

Try the batter.
Sweet. Luscious.
Listen to the lemons and blueberries collide,
the way they bind color with taste.
So much of life is in the Listening.

Layer a few blueberries across the top.
You know, the plump ones
that may burst across the peak
causing purple rippling
amidst the lemon almond cloud.

Ottolenghi calls for a glaze
but this is not necessary
as the cake is best bare,
with its purple blueberry veins showing.

Now carry it over to the house of your friend
in a basket, covered with a tea towel.
Let the scent of lemon open into their home.
Let the light envelop them.

Deborah Leipziger

COLD SOLACE

When my mother died,
one of her honey cakes remained in the freezer.
I couldn't bear to see it vanish,
so it waited, pardoned,
in its ice cave behind the metal trays
for two more years.

On my forty-first birthday
I chipped it out,
a rectangular resurrection,
hefted the dead weight in my palm.

Before it thawed,
I sawed, with serrated knife,
the thinnest of slices —
Jewish Eucharist.

The amber squares
with their translucent panes of walnuts
tasted — even toasted — of freezer,
of frost,
a raisined delicacy delivered up
from a deli in the underworld.

I yearned to recall life, not death —
the still body in her pink nightgown on the bed,
how I lay in the shallow cradle of the scattered sheets
after they took it away,
inhaling her scent one last time.

I close my eyes, savor a wafer of
sacred cake on my tongue and
try to taste my mother, to discern
the message she baked in these loaves
when she was too ill to eat them:

I love you.
It will end.
Leave something of sweetness
and substance
in the mouth of the world.

Anna Belle Kaufman

LAUNCH

I remember those airborne birds we painted
on my attic walls, the ones
my grandpa mistook for mustaches;
or my bedroom birds, the ones whose wings
my mom clipped so they could fly
Higher, safer.
Your dad was a pilot but math wasn't our thing;
we flung textbooks into afternoon air to see how their pages fared,
fluttered, our laughs louder
than our fears.
Bang trims and baked cookies; glitter high on cheekbones,
we launched each other into girlhood.
We once held hands at theme parks,
And on that ride when our feet came off the ground,
our ankles criss-crossing, Keds kissing,
your wrist rested on mine.
Your light was always on.
So when we released those lanterns into the Michigan sky,
our friendship soon fading into night
I kept my eyes on the flame propelling them forward, upward,
remembering then to remember now
Somewhere, we're still flying.

Nicole Schnitzler

IN A PAINTING BY VERMEER

It was my birthday when we met, both barely
out of childhood. I didn't have keys.
Sister unlocked you for me. I thought it strange,
in the hospital they liked to keep their prisoners
apart, restrained. You were in strips,
a mattress on the floor for fear of distress,
crouched in canvas I saw your wound.
Light drew bruise, pinned sapphires in your hair,
a girl in a painting by Vermeer.
I clothed you in weld, a turban of ultramarine
silk and a single pearl drop earring.
Sister shot the bolt.

I knelt beside you, your crime hung between us,
an underpainting bone black, you whispered,
He's dead. I killed him.
The police came twice but did nothing.
I was only trying to defend myself. How can I ever forgive myself?
I sat with your tears that fell like the rain
on the wild green earth above my house.
Sister returned.
I'd nothing to offer but a book and to say I'd be back.

Now, we are so much older and I'm ashamed I don't remember
what you got, though I think it was two for manslaughter.
Today another birthday, I carry you with me
to the wilds above my house.
No longer crouching or kneeling, we walk
following the silver skein of path
through meadow grass, cuckoo spit, rattle, clover.
Comfrey and vetch poultice our wounds.
We take off our turbans, let the morning wind free in our hair.

Avril Joy

ROAD TO WINDSOR

- *for Susan Hall Anthony, New England Writers co-founder (1940-2009)*

When I hold the dying woman, I feel the fierce spirit that has clung to earth
that bore her these long months of chemo and radiation: Her bones and skin
strong as the day she gave birth, limp as the night she lost her husband.

Come quickly, she says over the phone. *The liver*—as if someone else's—
has given out.

I pass Vermont farms, idle cattle, disinterested horse, man weed-whacking.
Drive past signs, *Amsden, 6 miles*. Curve with the road until the low maroon house
on Main Street. Door open.

She calls my name. There she is, shimmer and light, about to loose the body like an old nightgown. I offer useless prayer. Embrace her a second, last, time.
She holds on as if our spirits speak in dialogue no one can hear.

This mural-like existence no less than two women, a portrait, a Vermeer.
Love doesn't go away, I say. She knows. I put my hands at my heart
in *Namaste*, a gesture she returns.

Retrace route past the goat farm, old folks home, gas station, gravel pit.
More roadside red farms. Signs: *Maple syrup, fresh eggs, peas*.
Late afternoon uncombs goldenrod, lady slipper, purple cone.

Green hills home to sheep and dog, black-eyed Susans bright.
The envelope that folds in on itself,
daylilies that close at night.

Ann Cefola

SELF-ELEGY

Say she tried
   to wring tears from clouds
   hang them on a line of stars to dry
      poke holes in veils
      to unwed herself from lies
            leave more than breadcrumbs behind her

Say she never learned
   to walk on eggshells
   always cracking under her soles

Say she was stubborn
   sunk her teeth into forbidden apples
      juice dripping down her chin

It's okay to say
   she was afraid to die
   expecting neither angels nor brimstone
      though she worried
      the world's misery
            might imply a vindictive God

Say she'd be relieved
   to return as a sunflower
   or a seagull's wing dusting sky
      but not
            as a girl married off at twelve

Say she loved that every culture
   has its own tortilla and dumpling
   each language a different slice of moon

that she savored the seaweed she gathered
      still sighing its ocean breath
   that her laughter lightened over time
      though it carried the weight
            of broken branches

Say she kept believing
 most of earth's billions
 hold kindness under their tongues

Joanne Durham

WALKING WITH DOT

Sandsend to Whitby, January 11th 2020

Strong wind gusting on our backs:

we bless it, praise it, thank it
for its helpful, firm propulsion.

We feel the sand is blowing
as it rushes past our heels and ankles,

whipping-up like a locust swarm
or snaking like a pale murmuration.

We stride out, talking ten-to-the-dozen –
that easy chat of comrades – blind to the

sandstorm stinging the bare red cheeks
of walkers battling in the opposite direction.

We know the tide is coming in, realise
almost all is behind us, recognise inevitability,

but for a moment, we are safe, cushioned,
                                            warm.

Marilyn Longstaff

DURING THE PANDEMIC I LISTEN TO THE JULY 26, 1965, JUAN-LES-PINS RECORDING OF *A LOVE SUPREME*

The first familiar, know-them-anywhere notes bless me
this savage morning. Coltrane's horn racing
up and down every alley, in and out of veins and over the faces
of lakes and into the heart of stones.
And when he repeats *A love supreme* again and again,
It's as though, if he says it enough, he can ease
that mercy down into me, into the tiny ossicular chain,
the chemical rush, the spark, and my brain
getting it--if even just
for this thirty-two minutes and forty-eight seconds.
My daughter's been sick seven weeks with the virus.
Yesterday she felt a little bored, she texted. And I grab that
like a shopping cart. I load it up with hope.
Make it prayer. When the day's portion of the Torah is recited,
someone stands by to correct mistakes.
The words must vibrate precisely in the air.
So I open my door
to the breath of his instrument
that refuses nothing, lavishing the grass, gutters and trees,
concrete, cars, the gopher pulling down the new lettuces.
This generous sound that can mean
anything, nothing, whatever you need.
And isn't that god? Isn't that it?
This shivering? This fall to my knees?
Gods do walk among us.
But humans are, after all, a broken promise.
And yet, these humans seem to be trying
to enter...what?
I can almost hear it. This old planet.
Worms passing earth through their tissue.
Orchids, corn, mockingbirds throwing themselves into song
like there's no tomorrow. Which there may not be.
Yet, still a mountain. Still wind.
And Coltrane still offering the same four notes
like a teacher who is infinitely patient.

He's telling me it's worth it
to be in a body. He's telling me
I'm alive in a beach town in California and my daughter
in a high rise in Vancouver, my girl,
lying feverish on the couch she's been lying on
forty-nine days and forty-nine nights, still alive.

Ellen Bass

MEDICINE WOMAN

The attic sky is a sleeping green heart.
You've left your winter carapace at the door;
trace the kite of Auriga, the sturdy scent

of sage. The little pot-bellied stove warms
you with all the comfort of Bavaria,
gingerbread you'll chew to keep you from harm.

She brings terracotta pots, thumbed with lace,

to catch the salt water that melts from your
eyes, down the stone mountain that is your face.

And your breasts billow into doves of air.
She coaxes you alight with the coals at
the centre of her eyes; her hands, a small

cathedral in her lap, catch the rattle
of your dark. She unwraps a velvet mirage,
marked on the map by a charm of metal.

Here you will see your wounds are fans, large
and satin, you can open or close. And
you will survive, as a snake does. Forever.

For one hour, over and over, she can
be all the mothers you never had, all
the daughters you'll never carry, your sons.

She gives you, idiot child, an egg you'll
swaddle in the twisted silk of your hair.
Like a rope she rises. Like a rope pulled

away. You are naked as a peeled pear.
She eats you till you are just pips that will
sprout in loam, the luxury of your tears.

Linda France

NEW LOVE: A LIST

For Morgan

Chicago's river is frozen and I don't know its name.
Steam around the tops of skyscrapers.
Nisi means 'unless' in Latin. 13.1.16. Goodbye unless.
Old photographs on my phone I can't look at.
Coffee stains on a grey counter.
The ocean smell of your travel perfume,
the neckline of your blue t-shirt.
An indigo kettle whistles.
I have flown here suitcase half-full
chasing your strong arms and soft hands.
A song—hope-words—nouvelle, vague.
The pigeons ooo ooo ooo sound round.
Your snow boots are too heavy but the leather is beautiful.
Holding on. Holding on. Holding on.
A woman wearing black half-slides along an icy pavement.
I hope no-one's ever died for her.
Where can I buy tobacco from? And lipstick?
All the meals are designed for giants.
Wanting to ask everyone I've ever known if they are all right.
Remembering silence and silent treatments.
Thick gloves, hands-like-paws. Sub-Zero.
The bigness of greetings from strangers.
One says, *Get some size, girl!*
I am falling in Love with You. I am love-sized.
No one can ever tell me this is too soon.
Salt in shaker-sachets. Broken fragments of time.
Your mascara smear on the mirror.
Swipe-keys. Lights along corridor floors.
Every time I leave the room you think I'll disappear.
The river cracks into pale pieces and thaws dark again.
I always come back to the room that you're in.
Eighteen floors up and I'm watching the fire escapes—
wondering how long it takes to reach the ground, step by step.

Jess Richards

POETS

Ellen Bass. Among her poetry collections are *Indigo* (Copper Canyon Press, 2020), *Like a Beggar* (Copper Canyon Press, 2014), *The Human Line* (Copper Canyon Press, 2007), and *Mules of Love* (BOA 2002). Among her awards are Fellowships from the Guggenheim Foundation, The National Endowment for the Arts, The Lambda Literary Award, and four Pushcart Prizes. Her poems have appeared in *The New Yorker, The Atlantic, American Poetry Review, Poetry*, and many other journals. With Florence Howe, she co-edited the first major anthology of women's poetry, *No More Masks!* (Doubleday, 1973), and she co-authored the ground breaking, *The Courage to Heal: A Guide for Survivors of Child Sexual Abuse* (HarperCollins, 1988) and *Free Your Mind: The Book for Gay, Lesbian and Bisexual Youth—and Their Allies* (HarperCollins). A Chancellor Emerita of the Academy of American Poets, Bass founded poetry workshops at Salinas Valley State Prison and the Santa Cruz jails, and teaches in Pacific University's MFA program.

Cynthia Bernard is a woman in her early seventies who is finding her voice as a poet after many years of silence. A long-time classroom teacher and a spiritual mentor, she lives and writes on a hill overlooking the ocean, about 25 miles south of San Francisco. Her work has appeared in *Multiplicity Magazine, Heimat Review, The Beatnik Cowboy, The Journal of Radical Wonder, The Bluebird Word, Passager, Persimmon Tree, Poetry Breakfast, Verse-Virtual*, and elsewhere. She was selected by Western Rivers Conservancy to serve as the Poet-Protector of Deer Creek Falls in the northern Sierra Nevada foothills.

Eve West Bessier is a language enthusiast and an award-winning author. She is a poet laureate emerita of Silver City, New Mexico and of Davis, California. Her work is widely published, most recently in the *Los Angeles Review, El Palacio,* and *The Journal of Radical Wonder*. Eve is a monthly columnist for *Southwest Word Fiesta* (swwordfiesta.org). Her latest books are, *Pink Cadillacs: Short Stories* and *Poems Before Breakfast: Poetic Micro Essays*. Eve is an educator, jazz vocalist and nature photographer. She resides in Alamogordo, New Mexico. Find performance videos, photos, links to her books and more at her website: www.jazzpoeteve.com.

Rachel Burns was born in Newcastle Upon Tyne. She is published in magazines including *The Friday Poem, Ink, Sweat & Tears, Butcher's Dog, The Rialto, The Moth,* and *Magma*. Her short stories are published in *Signs of Life*, an anthology edited by Sarah Sasson, and *Mslexia*. She came second in The Julian Lennon Prize for Poetry 2021 and was longlisted in The National Poetry Competition 2021.

Ann Cefola is the author of When the Pilotless Plane Arrives (Trainwreck Press, 2021), Free Ferry (Upper Hand Press, 2017), and Face Painting in the Dark (Dos Madres Press, 2014); translator of Alparegho, like nothing else (Beautiful Days Press), forthcoming this year; The Hero (Chax Press, 2018), and Hence this cradle (Seismicity Editions, 2007); and recipient of the Robert Penn Warren Award selected by John Ashbery. For more information, see www.annogram.blogspot.com.

Barbara Crooker is author of twelve chapbooks and ten full-length books of poetry, including *Some Glad Morning*, Pitt Poetry Series, University of Pittsburgh Poetry Press, longlisted for the Julie Suk award from Jacar Press, *The Book of Kells* which won the Best Poetry Book of 2019 Award from Poetry by the Sea, and *Slow Wreckage* forthcoming from Grayson Books. Her other awards include: Grammy Spoken Word Finalist, the WB Yeats Society of New York Award, the Thomas Merton Poetry of the Sacred Award, and three Pennsylvania Council fellowships in literature. Her work appears in literary journals and anthologies, including *The Bedford Introduction to Literature*.

Monica Dobos was born in Romania and now lives in California with her family. She teaches Meditation and English online and is a substitute teacher for charter schools. This is her first published poem.

Joanne Durham is the author of *To Drink from a Wider Bowl,* winner of the Sinclair Poetry Prize (Evening Street Press 2022) and the chapbook, *On Shifting Shoals* (Kelsay Books 2023). She was a 2023 recipient of Third Wednesday Magazine's Annual Poetry Prize and the Mary Ruffin Poole Prize. A 2022 and 2023 Pushcart nominee, her poems appear in *Poetry South, Whale Road Review, Sky Island Journal, CALYX, Dodging the Rain,* James Crews' anthology, *The Wonder of Small Things*, and many other journals and anthologies. She lives on the North Carolina, USA coast, with the ocean as her backyard and muse. https://www.joannedurham.com/

Linda France's latest collections include Laurel Prize winner *The Knucklebone Floor* (Smokestack 2022) and *Startling* (Faber & New Writing North 2022), which includes work from her Writing the Climate residency with Newcastle University & New Writing North 2020-22. She won the 2013 National Poetry Competition and was Michael Marks Awards Environmental Poet of the Year 2022-23. Linda lives in Northumberland, close to Hadrian's Wall.

Jane Edberg is the author and artist of an illustrated memoir, *The Fine Art of Grieving*, published by Linen Press, 2024. She holds a Master of Fine Arts from the University of California, Davis and teaches writing at the Osher Lifelong Learning Institute at California State University at Monterey Bay. She offers writing workshops and works privately as a writing coach and editor. She serves as a contributing editor for *The Journal of Radical Wonder*. Her work is featured in the books, *Death, and its Terrible, Horrible, No Good, Very Beautiful Lessons: Field Notes from The Death Dialogues Project*; *My Dead*; *BAM 42 Stories* (to be released in 2024); and in many journals, including *Cholla Needles, MacQueen's Quinterly, and Gyroscope Review*. Jane resides in California next to the beautiful Monterey Bay National Marine Sanctuary. https://www.janeedberg.com/

Rebecca Faulkner is a London-born poet based in Brooklyn. The author of Permit Me to Write My Own Ending, (Write Bloody UK, 2023) her work appears in New York Quarterly, The Maine Review, The Poetry Society of New York, CALYX Press, Berkeley Poetry Review and elsewhere. She is a 2023 poetry recipient of the Barbara Deming Memorial Fund for Women, a finalist for the 2023 Desert Rat Poetry Prize, and the 2022 winner of Sand Hills Literary Magazine's National Poetry Contest. Rebecca was a 2021 Poetry Fellow at the Saltonstall Foundation for the Arts. She holds a BA in English Literature & Theatre Studies from the University of Leeds, an MA in Performance Studies from NYU, and a Ph.D. from the University of London. She is currently at work on her second collection of poetry, exploring female identity and artistic endeavour. www.rebeccafaulknerpoet.com

Beatriz F. Fernandez is a Miami area poet descended from Peruvian and Puerto Rican parents. She's the author of *The Ocean Between Us* (Backbone Press, 2017) and *Shining from a Different Firmament* (Finishing Line Press, 2015) which she presented at the Miami Book Fair. She has read her poetry on WLRN, South Florida's NPR news station and was the grand prize winner of the 2nd annual Writer's Digest Poetry Award. Her poems have been nominated for the Pushcart Prize three times in the last few years. IG: @nebula4291

Laura Foley is the author of ten poetry collections, including It's This and Why I Never Finished my Dissertation. She is a winner of the Narrative Poetry Contest, Good Books Poetry Contest, the Joe Gouveia Outermost Poetry Award, the Milton Kessler Award, the Atlanta Review Grand Prize, and the Bunner Medal from Columbia University, where she received an MA and an MPhil in comparative literature. She lives with her wife in West Lebanon, New Hampshire.

Shelly Eyre Graham is blessed to live in a renovated church in high desert Wyoming with her beloved husband and just the right amount of cats. She works as a psychologist and loves all things (& non-things) somatic, imaginal and depth psychological. A lifelong seeker, Shelly is eternally grateful for the practice of writing — especially poetry — as a means of self (& non-self) discovery.

Mare Heron Hake is a poet of the South Salish Sea, also known as Puget Sound in Washington State. Until recently, Hake was poetry editor, co-owner, and co-publisher for *Tahoma Literary Review* until her caregiving responsibilities took precedence. Mother of three very different individuals, a wife, feminist, and intentional crone, recent work can be found at Gyroscope Review, and is upcoming in 2024 as poetry contest finalist for Terrain.Org. Her two books were both published mid-pandemic without launches, but she loves them just the same. *SurvivalEye* (Arroyo Seco Press) and *Passages* (Xlibris) are both available through Amazon.com.

Stephanie Barbé Hammer is a 7-time Pushcart Prize nominee in fiction, nonfiction and poetry. She is the author of three poetry collections, two novels, a novelette, a new novella, and a how to write magical realism craft book. Originally from Manhattan, Stephanie moved to California in 1986, and except for a 7 year break in the PNW, has lived there ever since. She's a professor emerita of Comparative Literature at UC Riverside and she teaches writing at Hugo House and the Inlandia Institute. She loves palm trees, eavesdropping and walking to coffee.

Bonnie Hearn Hill is the author of sixteen traditionally published novels, numerous short stories and essays, and the poetry chapbook *Forgotten California*. Her poems have placed first in competitions including the Unitarian Universalist Awards, Chabot College Awards, and California State Poetry Society Awards, and her articles on writing have appeared in *Publishers Weekly, The Writer, Writer's Digest*, and other publications. She holds an MFA in Creative Writing from Antioch University Los Angeles and lives and writes in the Forgotten California of Fresno.

Andrea Hollander moved to Portland, Oregon, in 2011, after living for more than three decades in the Arkansas Ozarks, where she was innkeeper of a bed & breakfast for fifteen years and Writer in Residence at Lyon College for twenty-two. Hollander's sixth full-length collection is *And Now, Nowhere But Here* (Terrapin Books, 2023). Her fifth, *Blue Mistaken for Sky*, was a finalist for the Best Book Award in Poetry from the American Book Fest; her fourth, *Landscape with Female Figure: New & Selected Poems, 1982 – 2012*, was a finalist for the Oregon Book Award; her first,

House Without a Dreamer, won the Nicholas Roerich Poetry Prize. Her poems appear widely in journals, magazines, anthologies, and textbooks, including a feature in *The New York Times Magazine*. Other honors include two Pushcart Prizes and two poetry fellowships from the National Endowment for the Arts. In 2017, she established The Ambassador Writing Seminars, which she conducted in her home until the pandemic—now via Zoom. Her website is www.andreahollander.net.

Mary-Jane Holmes has won the Writer's Digest Rhyming Poetry Prize, Live Canon Poetry Pamphlet Prize, the Bath Novella-in-Flash Prize, the Bridport Poetry prize, Dromineer Flash Fiction Prize, Reflex Fiction Flash Fiction Prize and the Mslexia Flash prize. She has been shortlisted for the Beverley International Prize for Literature and longlisted for the UK National Poetry Prize twice. mary-janeholmes.com

Avril Joy's short fiction has appeared in literary magazines and anthologies, including Victoria Hislop's *The Story: Love, Loss & the Lives of Women*. Her work has been shortlisted in competitions including, the Bridport, the Manchester Prize for Fiction and The Raymond Carver Short Story Prize in the USA. In 2012 she won the inaugural Costa Short Story Award. *Sometimes a River Song*, published by Linen Press, won the 2017 People's Book Prize. Her poetry has also been widely published online and in poetry magazines, and in 2019 her poem *Skomm* won first prize in the York Literary Festival Competition.

Anna Belle Kaufman is a retired art psychotherapist, artist and writer who lives in Northern California. Her Pushcart nominated essays and poems have appeared in T*he Sun, Calyx, Utne Reader, The Plentitudes, The Networker*, and *Brain, Child magazine*.

Dragana Lazici lives in Cambridge, UK and has a complex background. Born in Romania to Serbian parents, she grew up in Montreal, Canada after her family escaped Communism. She then moved to London to do an MA in Applied Translation Studies in 2008. Her poetry often captures lived experiences of belonging to many places, from being a refugee and immigrant herself. Her first published poem was in Popshot Magazine in 2022. She was shortlisted for the Fiction Factory competition in 2023.

Yvonne Leach's second collection of poems *In the Spaces Between Us* hit the shelves this fall 2023, published by Kelsay Books. Her first collection *Another Autumn* was published by Cherry Grove Collections in 2014. She spent decades balancing a career in communications and public relations, raising a family, and pursuing her love of writing poetry. Her latest passion is working with shelter dogs. She splits her time living on

Vashon Island and in Spokane, Washington. For more information visit: www.yvonnehigginsleach.com

Deborah Leipziger is an author, poet, and advisor on sustainability. Born in Brazil, Ms. Leipziger is the author of *Story & Bone*, published by Lily Poetry Review Books. Her poems have been published in the UK, US, Canada, Mexico, Colombia, Israel and the Netherlands, in such magazines and journals as Pangyrus, Salamander, Lily Poetry Review, and Revista Cardenal. Her chapbook, *Flower Map*, was published by Finishing Line Press (2013). Deborah is a 2023-2024 Community Creative Fellow, selected by the Jewish Arts Collaborative. Ms. Leipziger has curated the New England Jewish Poetry Festival for 15 years. She serves as a Senior Fellow at the Institute for Social Innovation at Babson. A recipient of grants from the Massachusetts Cultural Council, Deborah has had residencies at T S Eliot House and Wellspring House.

Marilyn Longstaff lives in Darlington and is a member of Vane Women. Her residency at Hospitalfield in 2022, enabled her to finalise her sixth collection *Being Gemini*, which will be published by Smokestack Books in August 2024.

Ruth Mota lives in the Santa Cruz Mountains of California where she has retired to write poetry after a career as an international health trainer. Beside writing verse she also enjoys facilitating poetry circles to groups in her community like veterans or men in jail. Her poems have been published or are forthcoming in many online and print journals including *The Atlanta Review, Gyroscope Review, Terrapin Books, Quillsedge Press* and *Tulip Tree Press* among others.

Brenda Najimian Magarity lives in Fresno, California and is a second-generation Armenian American, daughter of a homemaker and a dry cleaner/hat blocker. When she was in her mid-20s, she became the driver for author William Saroyan. A former high school English teacher, she is a poet, writer and has served seven years as a member of the board for the Saroyan Society of Fresno. Her poetry has been online at *Armenian Poetry Project* and *The Anthology of Armenian Poets* (Volume II, updated 2014). Her poetry was included in *Armenian Town*. Najimian Magarity's essays have appeared in *William Saroyan: The Man and the Writer Remembered, The Fresno Bee, The California Courier*, and *The Chiron Review*. Her chapbook, *Carpet Weavers* will be published in the fall of 2024, by Finishing Line Press.

Andrea Potos is the author of seven full-length poetry collections, most recently *Her Joy Becomes* from Fernwood Press. A new collection from

Fernwood entitled *Belonging Songs* will be published in early 2025. Andrea's poems are published widely online and in print, including *The Sun, One Art, Midwest Quarterly, Braided Way, Poem, Poetry East, Potomac Review* and three anthologies from Storey Publishing including *How to Love the World: Poems of Gratitude and Hope*. She lives in Madison, Wisconsin, USA.

Stephanie Powell is a poet based in Melbourne. Her latest poetry collection is *Gentle Creatures* (Vagabond Press, 2023). She's been published in *Ambit Magazine, Acumen, The Rialto, Poetry Wales, The Moth* (IRE), *Cordite Poetry Journal* (AUS), *Rabbit* (AUS) and *Island Magazine* (AUS). She's the recipient of the 2022 Melbourne Poets Union Poetry Prize. In 2023 she was longlisted for the Winchester Poetry Prize. More info on her work can be found at: atticpoet.com

Lizzie Purkis is a British-born poet, who has made Chicago her home. While studying literature and modern languages at the University of St. Andrews, Scotland, she won the student poetry competition, and subsequently published poetry in North America and the UK, including *Scrivener, Verse*, and *Envoi*. Through various life stages, she kept returning to poetry, and was published most recently in the US in *Kerning | a space for words*, and *Of Rust and Glass*. She is a lifelong linguist, a social worker for humans across the lifespan, and a university lecturer teaching her craft to fledgling social workers. For glimpses go to: @kammermuse

Laura Ann Reed, a San Francisco Bay Area native, taught modern dance and ballet at the University of California, Berkeley before working as a leadership development trainer at the San Francisco headquarters of the United States Environmental Protection Agency. She and her husband now reside in western Washington. Her work has appeared in numerous American, British, and Canadian journals and anthologies. Her chapbook, *Shadows Thrown*, was published by Sungold Editions in 2023.

Jess Richards was born in Wales and raised in Scotland. She is the author of three literary fiction novels: Costa shortlisted *Snake Ropes, Cooking with Bones* and *City of Circles* (Sceptre). She also writes creative nonfiction, vispo, short fiction and poetry which have been published in various anthologies. Her fine art / creative writing PhD project, *Illusions, Transformations, and Iterations; storytelling as fiction, image, and artefact*, earned her a place on the Dean's List at Massey University, Aotearoa New Zealand. *Birds and Ghosts* (Linen Press) is a book-length work of creative nonfiction written when New Zealand borders were closed due to Covid19. In October 2022 Jess, her wife, and two stripy cats returned to live in the UK. They now live in Yorkshire where Jess works at the University of Leeds.

Belinda Rimmer came second in the Ambit Poetry Competition 2018, and the following year in the Stanza Poetry Competition. She has twice been shortlisted for the Laurie Lee Prize for Writing. Her pamphlet, *Touching Sharks in Monaco*, was a joint winner of the Indigo-First Pamphlet Competition, 2019. Her second pamphlet, *Holding On*, came out in November 2021 with New Walk Editions. And her chapbook, *How To Be Silent*, was published this year by dancing girl press.

Wendy Robertson. After a career in teaching and training teachers, Wendy Robertson transferred to full-time writing, having already written and published articles and stories. She has more than 20 novels and several collections of short pieces to her name. She has been inspired in her writing by travelling as far afield as France, USA, Russia, Spain and Singapore. She is also inspired by her life in South Durham whose history and identity she explores in many of her novels. Her love of history has led to her focus on some novels in celebrating the universality of family life and creativity in the midst of cruelty and kindness. The poem *Wind From the Sierra* emerged when she was writing *Long Journey Home*, a story about the Spanish Civil War.

Reshma Ruia is a British writer of Indian origin. Her first novel, Something Black in the Lentil Soup, was described in the Sunday Times as 'a gem of straight-faced comedy'. Her poetry collection, A Dinner Party in the Home Counties, won the 2019 Word Masala Award and her short story collection, Mrs. Pinto Drives to Happiness, was shortlisted for the 2022 Eastern Eye ACTA Awards. Her new novel, Still Lives has won the 2023 Diverse Book Readers' Choice Award and is selected for the 2023 Peoples Book Award. Reshma's work has appeared in anthologies and journals, and commissioned by the BBC, University of Cumbria and Manchester Literature Festival. She is the co-founder of The Whole Kahani – a writers' collective of British South Asian writers.
   www.reshmaruia.com
   @ReshmaRuia

Marjorie Saiser's eighth book, *The Track the Whales Make*, won the High Plains Book Award in 2022. Saiser's honors include the Willa Award for Poetry. Her poems have been published in *Poetry East, Midwest Quarterly, I-70 Review*, and *Rattle*, and can be found on her website:
   www.poetmarge.com.

Renée M. Schell's debut collection, *Overtones* was published in 2022 by Tourane Poetry Press. Her poetry appears in *New Verse News, Catamaran Literary Reader, Literary Mama, Naugatuck River Review*, and many other journals. She was lead editor for the anthology *(AFTER)life*: Poems and

Stories of the Dead. She earned a Ph.D. in German Studies and also taught for seven years at a Title I elementary school in San José, California. She shares her home with her family, four cats, and the spirit of Beethoven. You can find her at reneemschell.org.

Nicole Schnitzler is a Chicago-based writer who has written for publications such as *The Sun, The Chicago Tribune,* and *Esquire*. She is currently pursuing her MFA in creative writing and working on a memoir about family, faith, and the evolution of grief. She is also the founder of Doors Open Dishes, a nonprofit that partners with chefs to help keep the doors open to group homes and workshops for those with developmental disabilities.

Mary Anne Smith Sellen is a poet, painter, and bookseller. She has been widely published, both in print and online, also recognized in competitions, including 1st Sentinel Literary Quarterly November 2017, and 1st O Bheal Five Words Competition 2019. Her first full poetry collection *The shape of our lives* was longlisted in the 2023 Indigo Dreams First Collection competition. She is currently working on ideas for a new pamphlet. Mary Anne regularly reads at events and festivals in her home county of Kent and elsewhere.

Merna Dyer Skinner is a poet and communications consultant living in Portland, OR. Her poems have appeared in: *Gargoyle Magazine, ONE ART, Rust + Moth, Lily Poetry Review, Quartet,* and *The Baltimore Review*, among other journals, and three anthologies. Her chapbook, *A Brief History of Two Aprons*, was published by Finishing Line Press. Merna holds an MA in Communication Studies from Emerson College. She's lived in six US states, and travelled to six continents.

Mistee St. Clair has received a Rasmuson Foundation Individual Artist Award and an Alaska Arts and Literary Award, and has poems in *The Alaska Quarterly Review, The Common, Northwest Review, SWWIM Every Day*, and more. She lives with her family and border collie in a northern rainforest in Lingít Aaní (Juneau, Alaska), where she hikes, writes, wanders amongst the moss, and edits legislation for Alaska State Legislature. She can be found at misteestclair.com.

Laurel Szymkowiak is a poet from Western Pennsylvania. Her work has appeared in *Cagibi Literary Journal, Gyroscope Review, Twenty-two Twenty-eight, Pedestal Magazine,* and *Voices from the Attic* in addition to other publications. Her chapbook, *What Choir of Reality Will Sing Today?* received Honourable Mention in the Cutbank Chapbook contest, 2021. She is a regular participant in Madwomen in the Attic writing workshops.

Alison Stone is the author of nine full-length collections, *Informed* (NYQ Books, forthcoming), *To See What Rises* (CW Books, 2023), *Zombies at the Disco* (Jacar Press, 2020), *Caught in the Myth* (NYQ Books, 2019), *Dazzle* (Jacar Press, 2017), *Masterplan*, a book of collaborative poems with Eric Greinke (Presa Press, 2018), *Ordinary Magic*, (NYQ Books, 2016), *Dangerous Enough* (Presa Press 2014), and *They Sing at Midnight*, which won the 2003 Many Mountains Moving Poetry Award; as well as three chapbooks. Her poems have appeared in *The Paris Review, Poetry, Ploughshares, Barrow Street, Poet Lore*, and many other journals and anthologies. She has been awarded Poetry's Frederick Bock Prize and New York Quarterly's Madeline Sadin Award. She was Writer in Residence at LitSpace St. Pete. She is also a painter and the creator of The Stone Tarot. A licensed psychotherapist, she has private practices in NYC and Nyack. https://alisonstone.info/ YouTube and TikTok – Alison Stone Poetry.

Abigail Thomas has four children, twelve grandchildren, two great grandchildren, and a high school education. Her eight books include three works of fiction and *the memoirs Safekeeping; A three Dog Life; What Comes Next* and *How to Like It*; and most recently, *Still Life at Eighty: The Next Interesting Thing*. She lives with her dogs in Woodstock, NY.

Dara Yen Elerath's debut poetry collection, *Dark Braid* (2020, BkMk Press), won the John Ciardi Prize for Poetry. Her poems have appeared in venues such as *POETRY, the American Poetry Review, AGNI, POETS.org, Plume, Boulevard, High Country News* and *Poet Lore*, among others. She is an alumna of the Institute of American Indian Arts MFA in Creative Writing program and lives in Albuquerque, New Mexico.

ACKNOWLEDGEMENTS

Ellen Bass. "Indigo" and "The Orange-and-White-Heeled Shoes" from *Indigo*. Copyright © 2020 by Ellen Bass.
"Ode to Dr. Ladd's Black Slit Skirt" from *Like a Beggar*. Copyright © 2014 by Ellen Bass.
All reprinted with the permission of the The Permissions Company, LLC on behalf of Copper Canyon Press,
coppercanyonpress.org.
"During the Pandemic I Listen to the July 26, 1965, Juan-les-Pins Recording of *A Love Supreme*", *New England Review 2021*.

Joanne Durham. When My College Roommate Visited Peru was first published in *Gyroscope*, fall 2022. Self-Elegy was first published in *Sky Island Journal*, October 2023.

Linda France. *My Mother, the Sea* was previously published in *Storyville*, Bloodaxe 1997.

Homage to My Latin Teacher was previously published in *The Simultaneous Dress* Bloodaxe 2002.

Medicine Woman was first published in *The Gentleness of the Very Tall*, Bloodaxe 1994.

Ruth Mota. *Women Cooking Chicken* was published in *Passager Books* in 2018.

Laura Ann Reed.*The Sweetness* was first published in the journal *SWWIM*, Sep 30 2022.

Alison Stone. *First Pomegranate* appeared in *Ordinary Magic,* NYQ Books, 2016.

Merna Dyer Skinner. Pubescent Girls Fall in Love with Water Ballet first appeared in the New York University's journal Caustic Frolic, Volume 6, Issue 2, Fall 2021.

Marjorie Saiser. *The Track the Whales Make* and *The Sisters Play Cards in a Snowstorm* are from *The Track the Whales Make*, University of Nebraska Press, 2021.

Shelly Eyre Graham. *Riding Logos Waves* was first published in the Journal of Radical Wonder on May 31, 2023.

Marilyn Longstaff. *Gemini* was published in Dreich 2 magazine, *Walking with Dot* New Context 1 as *Premonition*.

Avril Joy. *Aztec Love Song for Women in Prison, In a Painting by Vermeer and In the Segregation Unit* were published in *Going in With Flowers*, Linen Press.

Brenda Najimian Magarity. *My Sister's Face* appeared in Armenian Town published by the William Saroyan Society in 2001.

Cynthia Bernard. *A Dream about my Mother* was originally published in *Heimat Review* in April, 2023.

Andreas Potos. *Final Poem for an Estranged Friend* appeared in the online journal *Headstuff* and *Marrow of Summer,* Kelsay Books.

Rachel Burns. *Parts of Flowers*, Spelt Magazine, Autumn 2021.

Barbara Crooker. *Lux Perpetua* is from *Slow Wreckage*, Grayson Books, 2024.

Mary-Jane Holmes. *The Waiting Room* and *On Botticelli's Primavera* are published in Mary-Jane's debut poetry collection *Heliotrope with Matches and Magnifying Glass* published by Pindrop Press.

Andrea Hollander.*The Color of the Sky* first appeared in *House Without a Dreamer,* Story Line Press, 1993.

Stephanie Barbé Hammer. *Naomie* was first published in *The Bridge E-Magazine* in July, 2023.

Reshma Ruia. Earlier versions of *New Me: Mother Me* and *A Conversation with Sylvia Plath* were published in *A Dinner Party in the Home Counties*, Reshma Ruia, Skylark Publications, 2019.

Laura Foley. *Little Darts* was published by Sunlight Press

Renée M. Schell. *Relativity* from *Overtones*. Copyright © 2022 by Renée M. Schell.

Rebecca Faulkner. Brighton Beach was first published in CV2 Magazine, and received an honorable mention for 2021 Foster Poetry Prize. It is included in her 2023 collection, Permit Me to Write My Own Ending.

Yvonne Leach. *duty* originally appeared in Phantasmagoria Magazine.

Deborah Leipziger. *How to Help a Friend Mourn* was previously published in the *San Pedro River Poetry Review*, Fall, 2022.

Anna Belle Kaufman. *Cold Solace* was published in Sun Magazine, September, 2010.

Nicole Schnitzler. This is the print debut of Schnitzler's poem *Launch*.

Ann Cefola. *Road to Windsor* first appeared in *Face Painting in the Dark*, Dos Madres Press, 2014.

Wendy Robertson. *Winds from the Sierra* was published in *Kaleidoscope*.

www.ingramcontent.com/pod-product-compliance
Lightning Source LLC
Chambersburg PA
CBHW042129100526
44587CB00026B/4226